American Zeitgeist is a narrative in verse about the footnote, statesman William Jennings Bryan. Bryan was a Populist Democrat, a true man of the people, who remains the only candidate to run for, and lose, three times, the election for president of the United States. Despite planting the seeds for Progressive policies, as a man who honored the spirit and tenor of American Democracy, Bryan is mostly remembered for being on the wrong side of history. As a man of deep religious conviction and a dynamic public orator, his defense of Creationism in the infamous Scope Trial, marked him forever as a reactionary crank. Rammelkamp gives us a much larger context to consider the man's life and work. May our best poets continue to write our history.

—Alan Catlin, poet, author of *American Odyssey*

Is it a bird (read "poem")? Is it a plane (read "novella"): YES. It is Charles Rammelkamp's latest history-rooted poetry collection, this one based on William Jennings Bryan's rise and fall as an American hero—from hero to buffoon, in H. L. Mencken's words. The book is even a suspense story, with a good little surprise at the end. I am fond of poetry collections which might appeal to people who dislike poetry: this one surely will. But if you do like poetry, or at least language that's magical, you will find memorable imagery. I, for one, will hear the simile "June (at the Scopes trial) leaning on us like a schoolyard bully" every time local humidity smacks me in the face. If poetry is called upon to "teach and delight," as Horace and Sir Philip Sidney tell us, then AMERICAN ZEITGEIST fills the bill, teaching in a most delightful way how the political scene surrounding William Jennings Bryan parallels that of 2016. It may actually help us find a place in our minds for our own milieu.

— Clarinda Harriss, Publisher, BrickHouse Books, Co-Editor, with Moira Egan, of *HOT SONNETS; AN ANTHOLOGY*; author of *THE WHITE RAIL: Stories*

Within *American Zeitgeist*, Charles Rammelkamp invites readers to inhabit the world of William Jennings Bryan, relive significant historical episodes from his remarkable life. Foreshadowing our current landscape of political populism, this collection of poetry documents the rise and fall of a larger-than-life personality, brought down by his own fatal flaw.

> — Jennifer Lagier, author of *Harbingers* (Blue Light Press) and *Scene of the Crime*, co-winner of the *Evening Street Press* Helen Kay Poetry Chapbook Prize.

Endlessly inventive, this Charles Rammelkamp. Who would think the life and times of William Jennings Bryan would be the stuff of top-notch verse? *American Zeitgeist* is a brave testament to a figure who still resonates today. But the real bravery here is Rammelkamp's—what a tour-de-force of voice, and carefully constructed historical reimagining. Bravo!

> — Nathan Leslie, author of nine books of fiction including *Root and Shoot, Sibs, Drivers.* and the novel, *The Tall Tale of Tommy Twice.s*

American Zeitgeist

AMERICAN ZEITGEIST

Charles Rammelkamp

Apprentice House
Baltimore, Maryland

Copyright © 2017 by Charles Rammelkamp

All rights reserved. No part of this book may be reproduced or transmitted in form or by any means, electronic or mechanical, including photocopy, recording, or any information storage and retrieval system, without prior permission from the publisher (except by reviewers who may quote brief passages).

First Edition

Printed in the United States of America
Paperback ISBN: 978-1-62720-151-3
E-book ISBN: 978-1-62720-152-0

Design by Patrick Schillig

Published by Apprentice House

Apprentice House
Loyola University Maryland
4501 N. Charles Street
Baltimore, MD 21210
410.617.5265 • 410.617.2198 (fax)
www.apprenticehouse.com
info@apprenticehouse.com

This book is dedicated to Eric, Ellen, David, TC, Shad, Oliver, Ken, Fred, Neil, Barbara and all Illinois College alumni, the seeds of my interest in this subject of fiction and history. Also to my aunt, Jane Highsaw, who sat on Bryan's knee once long ago.

"One somehow pities him, despite his so palpable imbecilities. It is a tragedy indeed to begin life as a hero and to end it as a buffoon."

> —H.L. Mencken, July 16, 1925 at the Scopes Trial
> in Dayton, Tennessee

Contents

Foreword xiii

Progressive 1

History 102, Illinois College 3
Before 5
Promise 6
The Deacon 7
Like Father Like Son 9
Revival 11
Jefferson Powers' Jealousy 13
Marriage 15
WJB and the Jail for Angels 16
Jefferson Powers' Own Prison 18
Won and One 20
Itching to Run 22
Oratory 23
The Voice that Launched a Thousand Nightmares 25
Lincoln 27
Conceding Defeat 29
Moral Reform and Political Expediency 31
Willy Goes to Washington 32
Power to the People 34
Running for Reelection 36
Progressive 37
Blinded Ambition 39
Mary's Request 40
The Panther 41

Cross of Gold 43

The Silver Dagger 44
Conventional Wisdom 46
Showdown 48
Cross of Gold 49
Nomination 52
On the Stump 53
Election Results 55
Schadenfreude 57
The Gadfly 59
The House on D Street 61
The Two-Sided Desk 62
Professor Lynn and the Wizard of Oz 64
WJB on Maine and Spain – and Ill-Gotten Gain 66
War Is a Terrible Thing 68
Willy's War 70
The War over Imperialism 71
Renomination 72
In God We Trust 74
The Rematch 75
WJB Reflects on His Loss 76
Blood on His Hands 78
Jefferson Lynn Lectures about TR and WJB 80
The Great Commoner Unbound 81
Public Enemy Number One 83
European Tour 84
The Rise of Roosevelt 86
Chautauqua 87
Tainted Money 89

Fool's Gold 91

A Trip Around the World 92
The Men from the Press Said We Wish You Success 94

The Squarest Christian 96
Three Strikes 98
Temperance 100
Kingmaker 101
Two Cats 103
WJB Declares Victory 105
Give Peace a Chance 107
Mary Takes It Hard 109
John Reed Interviews The Great Commoner 111
He Kept Us Out of War 113
War 115
What It Means to Be Patriotic 117
Prohibition 119
Age and Illness 120
Illness and Age 122
The Menace of Darwinism 123
When I'm Sixty-five 125
Local Interest 127
Rhea County Courthouse 129
Monkey Business 130
Willy in the Jungle 131
Intermission 132
The Monkey House 133
Humiliation 134
Willy Denounces Darrow in the Name of God 137
Fool's Gold 138
After 139
Charlotte Biggs' Legacy 141
Footnote 143
Biographical Note 145

American Zeitgeist • Rammelkamp — xiii

Acknowledgments

I'd like to acknowledge the professional work of the Apprentice House staff led by Kevin Atticks, and including Luisa Beguiristain, Mary Del Plato, Ellen Haynie and Patrick Schillig.

The poem "After" appeared in Prairie Winds, and the following poems appeared in *Syndic Literary Journal*: "Cross of Gold," "Blood on His Hands," "Tainted Money," "The Men from the Press Said We Wish You Success," "When I'm Sixty-five" and "Fool's Gold." Thanks to LeRoy Chatfield, editor.

The following books were invaluable in my research:

> *Bryan: A Political Biography of William Jennings Bryan* by Louis W. Koenig
>
> *A Godly Hero: The Life of William Jennings Bryan* by Michael Kazin
>
> *Anti-Intellectualism in American Life* by Richard Hofstadter

I would like to thank my friend Robert Cooperman for reading and commenting on this manuscript; his comments and suggestions improved this book. I'd also like to acknowledge my wife, Abby, for helping maintain a family environment that makes this kind of work possible.

Foreword

Had he not died within a week from the conclusion of the Scopes trial in which he was made a national laughingstock, I have no doubt that William Jennings Bryan would have staged another Nixonian comeback and replaced the impression the nation had of him with yet another, though perhaps even less flattering. Already he was preparing speeches to vindicate himself, and certainly his dubious cause in the famous Tennessee trial, Creationism, has its adherents to this day. In any case, Bryan was always the example that gave the lie to F. Scott Fitzgerald's observation that there are no second acts in American lives.

No doubt his comeback would be in the service of some other symbolic, largely futile cause, but perhaps he'd have redeemed himself, or at least put the memory of his shame in the rearview mirror. He was the Don Quixote of the Prairie, forever tilting at windmills.

The old saw that history is written by the victors is so true, and Bryan was seldom a winner. In the Populist tradition of which he was the classic champion, he stood in futile defense of the "little guy," speaking truth to power. Thus, despite thirty years of helping to shape the American narrative, he is little more than a footnote today. In a world where thirty percent of Americans are unable to name the current Vice President and a quarter are not able to name the country from which the United States gained its independence, it's not surprising that Bryan is largely forgotten, an obscure figure in American History courses.

My grandfather, who died twenty years before I was born, was acquainted with Bryan, when he was president of Illinois College, Bryan's alma mater. Bryan, who graduated from Illinois College in 1881, was on the board of trustees at the time. This is the true source of my interest in Bryan.

Bryan resigned from the board of trustees in 1905 when the college accepted money from Andrew Carnegie. Bryan believed colleges were "selling out" to the plutocrats when they accepted their money. "Our college cannot serve God and Mammon," he wrote in his letter of resignation. "It cannot be a college for the people and at the same time commend itself to the commercial highwaymen."

The grant from Carnegie enabled the college to survive. If it ever sold out to anything, it was not the plutocrats. Bryan also said in 1924 to the Seventh-Day Adventists, "All of the ills from which America suffers can be traced back to the teaching of evolution. It would be better to destroy every other book ever written, and save just the first three verses of Genesis." So maybe the college was better off without the anti-intellectual's support after all.

—Charles Rammelkamp

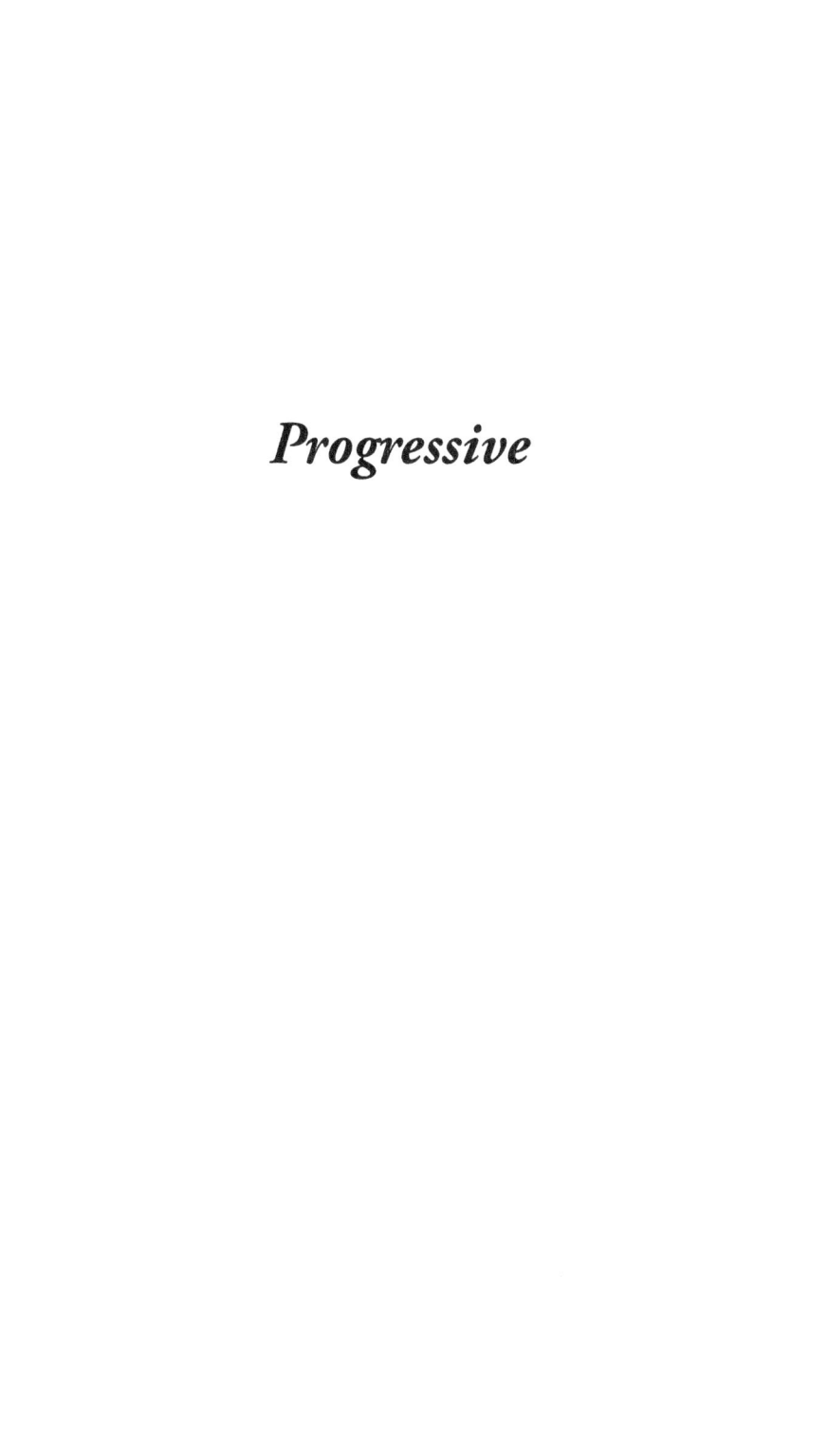

Progressive

History 102, Illinois College

We'd just chugged into the Progressive Era,
second semester American History survey,
spring in the air, winter retreating from the prairie
like the defeated Confederate army,
Reconstruction and Carpetbaggers in the South,
American expansion and Indian wars in the West,
all in the rearview mirror, behind us now.

"That great Phi, William Jennings Bryan,"
Professor Lynn began his lecture,
when all the students had settled in their seats,
looking pointedly at Jeremy Babcock,
president of the Sigma Pi fraternity,
archrival of Phi Alpha,
"three times the Democratic candidate
for the presidency, the youngest ever to run."

"Professor Lynn!" Babcock waved his hand,
knowing Lynn was yanking his chain,
playing along with the professor.
"Professor Lynn! Sir! Doctor Lynn!"

"Yes, Mister Babcock?"

"Professor Lynn, Bryan was a Sig!" Babcock declared.
He could have been Patrick Henry vowing
"Give me liberty, or give me death!"

Smiling to himself, Lynn strutted
in front of the blackboard in Crispin Hall,
shaking his head as if at a private joke.

"Yes, Mister Babcock," he said after a dramatic pause,
"Bryan belonged to Sigma Pi
when he attended Illinois College,
but why anyone would want to admit it
is beyond me."

Before

I knew him before
he was a hero or a buffoon,
before he was anybody
but Willy Bryan, a farm kid,
though his sober-faced daddy, Silas,
the circuit court judge
and just this far from being elected
to the House of Representatives in Washington
(and ever impatient with drunks,
like my father, Caleb Powers),
ruled like an Olympian in Salem,
Marion County's county seat,
and his ma, Miz Mariah,
came from one of the oldest
families in the county, the Jennings clan.

One of nine kids, three dead
before they turned five, a younger brother
going to his grave at seventeen,
Willy came into the world
a year before it turned upside down,
March, 1860, just months before
Abe Lincoln's election.

Promise

When the earth shook New Madrid, Missouri,
ringing church bells as far away as Boston
and like some command from God
making the mighty Mississippi flow backwards,
Captain Sam Young fled like Noah in his ark
in search of safer ground.
He sank his roots here,
Noah's dove coming to rest,
in the rich soil of Salem, Illinois.

A decade later the drought up north
sent wagonloads of folks in search of grain,
like the Hebrews in Joseph's day to Egypt,
so they dubbed our land Little Egypt:
Salem's the Gateway to Little Egypt.

So you could say Salem's nothing
if not a place of salvation.
Willy Bryan knew that better than most,
inspired to find redemption
in a way of living,
spread that message
to all who would heed
the promise.

The Deacon

Silas Bryan sent a load of hay
to every preacher in town,
come time for haying,
even though he was a Baptist.
Mariah followed the Methodists,
and Willy went to both.

No matter the denomination,
they all condemned dances,
circuses, theater, gambling,
and especially alcohol.

One day I'll never forget,
my daddy lay in the gutter,
sleeping off a drunk.
Mama'd sent me to fetch him.

Silas and Willy passed by,
stepping wide around him,
as if to avoid infection.
Silas, who'd been state senator,
elected superintendent of schools, too,
shook his head at my pa,
pitying, disgusted.

With the reflex of breath or blinking
Silas grunted his disapproval,
muttered the single word, "drunk,"
as if he wanted to vomit.
In that instant Willy and I
caught each other's eye,
and then both were gone,
only a tang of righteousness in the air.

"Pa!" I cried, shaking his shoulder,
not sure if I was embarrassed or angry,
at Willy or Pa.
"Pa! Come on! Ma needs you home!"

Like Father Like Son

Willy whetted his taste for politics
on his father's toothsome run
for the U.S. House of Representatives.
Twelve at the time,
Willy attended all the campaign rallies,
as if rich banquets,
gorged on the speeches,
no doubt dreamed
like a kid in a candy shop
his own future feasts.

Inspired, Willy joined
the Salem high school debating club,
already in love with the power
of the spoken word –
as much in religion as politics.

A Democrat like his daddy,
Willy supped on Silas' Jacksonian principles:
The government that's best
is the one that governs the least.

Silas lost
though the outcome was close,
Democrats painted as the party
that killed the Union soldiers,
Republicans claiming a monopoly on patriotism.

Silas raged against Lincoln's Emancipation Proclamation,
claiming Lincoln'd turned the war
from a preservation of the Constitution
to "a free negro crusade."
The South had erred in seceding, he said,
but nobody in Little Egypt voted for Lincoln.

Silas came within just a few votes
of being elected – bitter consolation.
In defeat he set the example
Willy would follow to his grave.

Revival

Churches went on a tear in the Seventies,
saving souls in the name of Jesus
all across small-town America.
With the war fading into memory
like a dimming bad dream,
they must have felt
the way a person does waking up
from a deep self-forgetful sleep:
a disoriented urgency propelling them forward,
headlong into some poorly thought-out action.
The Baptists, the Presbyterians, the Methodists –
they all had their angles –
immersion, conversion, second blessing.

Willy's "spiritual rebirth" arrived
like a train pulling into a station,
a powerful engine governed by a timetable,
like a boy's first crush
when his voice cracks, hairs sprout all over.

.He was fourteen then, still living in town,
but he didn't seem any different to me:
He'd always looked in horror
at "improper conduct,"
trained by his ma and pa to disdain frivolity –
dancing, joking, horsing around.
So his revival just seemed like
more hymn-singing and sermons to me.

Still, I heard him once
telling Roddy Willis
Christ was committed to everybody
who accepted him as Savior.
My pa'd just died from the drink,
and I wanted nothing more
than to punch Willy's smug face.
It gave me a reason to continue, at least,
why I decided to become a writer.

Jefferson Powers' Jealousy

Willy's success goaded me on
like spurs in a horse's flanks –
a self-inflicted bite of ambition,
to somehow out-do him:
I was doomed from the start.
Though a year younger,
he always beat me at debate,
even though he'd only been two years in school,
his mama teaching him his lessons
until he was ten.

When Silas sent him to Whipple Academy,
the Illinois College prep school in Jacksonville,
I thought I was shut of him at last.
"A typical farm lad with all the crudities
characteristic of the species,"
one professor later recalled.

But news of Willy's triumphs traveled
back to Egypt, galling me for the advantages
he'd started with; my pa just a drunk,
us a dirt poor Salem family.
He edited the school newspaper,
delivered the valedictory address
to the graduating class of 1881,
got hitched to Mary Baird,
top student at the Jacksonville Female Academy.
The only cloud in his sunny blue sky
Silas' stroke and death from diabetes
the year before Willy graduated.

Bryan became the white whale
to my Captain Ahab.

Marriage

Silas' death dashed Willy's hopes
to study at Oxford a year
before starting law school,
but his run of luck continued
when he won Mary Baird,
the dazzling princess of the Jacksonville Female Academy.
I saw her once or twice
when she came to Salem,
bright, flashing eyes,
an oval face and small mouth,
brimming with humor and life:
probably the perfect wife –
I heard she was Willy's best companion.

Me, I married a girl from Centralia,
Charlotte Biggs, by name,
a buxom blond girl,
just as I'd started
as a reporter for the Salem *Sentinel*.
I felt at last my good fortune
matched Willy J. Bryan's –
the stars now shone as bright on me
as they ever had on him –
until a couple years later,
Willy still studying law
at Union Law School in Chicago,
Charlotte ran off with a fellow
she'd known before me in Saint Louis.

WJB and the Jail for Angels

I fell for Mary Baird the moment I saw her
at the tea-and-cookie reception that autumn afternoon
at the Jacksonville Female Academy,
what we Illinois College boys called
the Jail for Angels,
the regulations for consorting with the girls so strict
they might as well have been in a convent,
watched over by nuns,
strapped into chastity belts,
secured in a castle without a key.

Sharp as the spines of an Osage Orange,
witty and brilliant, so easy to admire,
those kind gray-brown eyes
bathed me with their warmth
like a Baptism of love.

Mary didn't fall for me, though,
saw me as a boy with a halo
since I didn't smoke or drink or dance.
But, persistent, I finally wore her down.

Thank goodness for Mrs. Tanner,
the IC Latin professor's wife,
for allowing me to visit her once a week,
when Mary just happened to come to her parlor, too.
But my boldness got the better of me,
and when I took her riding in a rented buggy,
stern old Mr. Bullard, the JFA principal,
suspended Mary for the rest of that spring term.
How crushed I felt; all my fault.

Bullard sent Mary home,
took her to the train station himself.
But I'd sneaked onto the baggage car
without anybody knowing,
surprised Mary at her seat.
We exchanged the rings we wore that day –
June 4, 1880.

Jefferson Powers' Own Prison

I felt my luck had finally changed
when I met Charlotte Biggs at the Steenkamps',
Earl an editor for the *Sentinel,*
where I'd just started as a reporter,
his wife Mabel a cousin of Charlotte's.

By the way I sold myself to Charlotte,
a gorgeous young woman from Centralia,
I must have dazzled her
with the glamorous vision of journalism –
interviewing governors and opera singers,
reporting on presidential politics –
when in reality, after we were married,
I was just out all the time, home late,
hungover half the time
from hanging out in saloons
looking for stories.

Charlotte became a block of ice
I chopped at and chopped at,
unable to get her to thaw.
Even when she came with me to Springfield,
a dinner at the governor's mansion for all the hacks,
she still wouldn't forgive me.

What Charlotte wanted all along
was a quiet life of anonymity,
which she finally found
when she visited her folks back home
and ran into an old classmate,
Douglas Lynn, a St. Louis schoolteacher
with whom she eloped
a week before our third anniversary.

Won and One

It wouldn't be for five years
since I met her at the tea-and-cookies reception
that I'd make Mary mine at last.

I'd already asked Mister Baird for his daughter's hand,
but after Pa died –
a stroke at the age of fifty-seven;
he'd come to Jacksonville from Salem
for his diabetes,
all set to meet my Mary,
when it happened –
I had to make sure
I could take care of us first,
so I went to law school in Chicago
after I graduated from Illinois College.
Pa'd always planned to send me to Oxford for a year
but we just didn't have the money after he died.

Once I got my law degree,
I set up practice back in Jacksonville,
my first client a saloonkeeper
for whom I collected debts.
I let Sheehan know I didn't drink,
but I told him I thought anybody
who bought liquor ought to pay for it.
Soon I began collecting for Illinois College, too:
the number of my clients grew.

At last, on October 1, 1884,
my former Latin professor, Edward Tanner,
now president of Illinois College,
married me and Mary
at her parents' home in Perry.
On Mary's wedding band I inscribed:
"Won, 1879. One, 1884."

Itching to Run

Will married Mary after law school,
setting up practice back in Jacksonville,
but what he really wanted was to run for office,
like his Democrat daddy, Silas.

But he could never get elected to office
a Democrat in Jacksonville,
central Illinois about as Republican
as Egypt was Democrat.
He was out of place, restless
as a Protestant in a Catholic church.

I heard he tried to get a patronage position
from the Cleveland administration
but without any luck.
Willy volunteered at the church,
took part in temperance activities –
oh, he continued to speak out
against the evils of alcohol, all right --
but still he was antsy as a pup,
needed to move on.

I reported all this in the *Sentinel* –
the local boy makes good.

"That Willy Bryan," people'd say.
"He's sure to make something of himself."

"Yep," I'd bite off the grudging response.

Oratory

Willy always had a flair for speechifying.
His valedictory address at Illinois College,
a simple-minded address on "Character,"
portraying life as a choice between good and evil –
the sort of thing an earnest eighth-grader might declaim,
elaborating on the person shining from the soul
"either as a beam of purity
or as a clouded ray that betrays the impurity within."
Embarrassing, really.
His professors must have groaned,
smiled politely as Willy delivered his address
like a boy playing
some old-time senator in the Roman Republic.

Back in Jacksonville with Mary –
after law school and marriage –
Willy was president of the YMCA
and coached Illinois College kids
in his literary society, Sigma Pi,
their oratory skills.

Willy's favorite topic?
Prohibition, of course.
Sure he could uplift their humanity
through the power of his golden tongue,
he bullied country audiences
about the evils of drink,
urging them to sign abstinence pledge cards.

"The saloon is open all the time,"
he warned, hysterical as a schoolgirl,
"wickedness never tires; vice never sleeps."

The Voice that Launched a Thousand Nightmares

Willy could have been an actor,
intoning Shakespeare's words on stage,
a raging, anguished Hamlet, a thundering Othello,
any of the Kings Henry, a mad, mad Lear.
Or he could have been a preacher,
pronouncing his prophetic disapproval
of the evils of alcohol and gambling,
threatening divine retribution for sin;
crooning soothing promises of salvation,
fantasies of an Afterlife,
in that deep, majestic baritone.

He chose instead to be a lawyer,
then a politician and public speaker,
earning his way on his oratory,
supporting a family with his vocal cords.

Again I'd hoped I was shut of him
when he left Jacksonville,
settling his wife and their daughter Ruth
in distant Nebraska, which still seemed to me
a remote territory in 1888,
even though a state for twenty years,
choosing the capital, Lincoln, to practice law in.

But soon the news of his legal success,
swaying the juries with that persuasive voice,
traveled back to his hometown,
and then he began to make campaign speeches
on behalf of the Democratic party,
drumming up clients for his practice
with the magnificent addresses with which
he stirred up the crowds.

Yes, we heard all about him back in Salem,
and I dutifully reported the news in the *Sentinel*,
but face it, he'd never really left me.
His was the voice that spoke
in my loneliest midnight dreams,
taunting me, challenging me, scorning me.
"*A drunk*," I'd hear him mock,
drowning in my troubled sleep.

Lincoln

I was getting nowhere in Jacksonville.
Four years running errands for the party,
I still couldn't get nominated
for any local office, and besides,
a Democrat had no chance winning in that town.

Tried to get an appointment as assistant DA
over in Springfield, figuring
my chances good with Cleveland in the White House,
and me a loyal Democrat,
but nobody gave me the time of day.

So when I went west to Kansas
to collect overdue interest for Illinois College,
I came home by way of Lincoln, Nebraska,
where I spent a weekend with Adolphus Talbot,
an old law school friend.

Adolphus was big on Lincoln,
told me that with my oratory skills
I had a bright future as a trial lawyer
there in Lincoln –
on the frontier but still four times
the size of Jacksonville.
Adolphus proposed we form a partnership.

Back home, I told Mary.
"You know Jacksonville," she said,
shrewd as a wise and loyal wife,
intimate with my ambition,
alive to my frustration.
"You have seen Lincoln.
If you think a change is for the best,
I am willing to go."

Conceding Defeat

Nebraska Democratic party leaders
approached Bryan to run for the House in 1890
as if courting a virgin.
He wasn't even thirty when they started their wooing.
His silver tongue moved the masses,
just what the party needed.

"Last night I found that I had power
over the audience," he told his devoted Mary
after one campaign rally.
"I could move them as I chose."
He prayed for divine guidance
like a Biblical prophet leading the faithful.
Should he or shouldn't he?
But he could Hamletize all he wanted –
it was clear what answer he'd get from God.

Word traveled down to Salem
like the wind blowing west to east,
and of course I reported the news
of Willy's nomination in the *Sentinel.*

Now I knew he'd bettered me.
He was in the big-time now,
playing a role on the national stage,
in the thick of regional politics.

In a way it came as relief,
conceding defeat to my private rival.
Nobody knew but me,
though the shame was no less humiliating.
I'd have been laughed out of Salem
if I'd ever told anybody.

Moral Reform and Political Expediency

"The man who drinks
not only is unwise but *sins,*"
Willy'd written when he lived in Jacksonville,
"He sins against himself, against those
dependent on him, against society,
and against God…"

But in Nebraska, the Irish, Germans and Poles
who made up the party opposed prohibition,
and Willy, convincing himself of the truth
of ideological arguments about personal liberty,
with an eye to his constituency,
though supporting temperance as a virtue
akin to brotherly love
and abstaining from alcohol as if from poison,
ran on a platform opposing laws that affect
"the social habits of the people."
A hypocrite? A convincing one, at least.
For a time I too believed
that *he* believed in personal liberty.

I grudgingly admired Willy's political finesse,
his adroit campaign,
skirting the prohibition issue.
Fear-mongering opponents pointed out
the inconsistency between his lifestyle
and his platform, but he convinced enough voters
to win the election and go to Washington,
succeeding where Silas had failed.

Willy Goes to Washington

In the *Sentinel* we reported
the birth of the Bryans' third child, Grace,
shortly after their arrival in Washington,
another reminder of my lonely bachelorhood,
the long-lost Charlotte Biggs –
Charlotte *Lynn,* I mean, her new married name.

But Willy didn't do much
his first legislative session:
he was just biding his time,
studying the tariff and currency issues.

They thought him a hayseed at first,
a pushover hick from the plains,
but his political savvy soon won him
a place on the powerful Ways and Means committee
when he cozied up to the Speaker of the House,
supporting William Springer like a cheerleader
for the hometown football squad.
Now he had the chance to use his powerful voice.

Mary worked with him on his speeches,
following public policy issues like a bloodhound,
sending secret signals to Will
from the visitors' gallery
when her husband rose to speak on the floor,
nodding approval, shaking her head in warning.
A real team. Though almost a decade
since Charlotte had left me for her St. Louis fancy man,
I almost choked on my envy,
hearing these tales of matrimonial harmony.

I can still see the story in the *Sentinel* –
March of 1892 –
Will's first major floor speech.
He spoke for over three hours
on a proposal to reduce the wool tariff,
filling the chambers with the spellbinding cadence
of his eloquent voice.
Not just the *Sentinel*, even the New York newspapers
splashed his name and speech across the front pages,
insuring his fame, securing his influence.

Power to the People

Willy fought for his constituents that first term
like a crusader for Christ,
introducing bills with the people in mind:
direct election of U.S. Senators
instead of letting state legislatures decide;
fighting trusts and monopolies
with the weapons of tariff reductions;
requiring publicity for federal court orders
foreclosing land mortgages;
befriending members of the Populist party.
The consummate insider outsider.

Populists were big back in Nebraska,
Willy of a like mind.
Favored a graduated income tax,
women's suffrage, an eight-hour work-day,
government ownership of the railroads;
re-shaped the Democratic party –
modifying its Jacksonian principles:
now advocating the best government
is the one with policies to promote equality,
fairness for the common man.

"I shall go forth to the conflict
as David went to meet
the giant of the Philistines,"
he promised when nominated,
"not relying on my own strength
but trusting the righteousness of my cause."

What a cornball!
But my goodness, was he dedicated!

Running for Reelection

I never had a head for money;
I could never follow the arguments
about gold versus silver,
like a path that goes through the woods
only an Indian scout could track,
leaving me lost, not knowing where to turn,
but Willy claimed that silver coinage
stabilized the value of money
through inflationary action.

His was an argument for the common man,
he claimed, to keep him from being cheated
by the big money boys who ruled the roost;
but Nebraska Democrats took sides
with the conservative views of President Cleveland.

So Willy chose to speak out his own views,
stressing tariff and income tax issues,
instead of toeing the party line,
in a district where Republicans outnumbered Democrats.

But the Populists supported him,
and in the candidates' debate,
Willy's eloquence swayed the people like Mark Antony:
he talked circles around his opponents,
won a second term on the power of his voice.

Progressive

"Bryan was a Democrat
when the good guys were the Republicans,"
Professor Lynn lectured, strutting
before the blackboard in Crispin Hall,
pausing now and then
to glance at his notes on the lectern.

"But he helped his party become
the advocates for the helpless,
I'll give him that much.

"First leader of any major party –
any major party –"
Lynn paused, stared us down
as we lounged in our student chairs,
pens poised over notebooks,
scribbling his observations.

"…to argue for the federal government
to provide for the welfare
of ordinary Americans –
working class, middle class –
the welfare of *ordinary* Americans."

He could have been a courtroom lawyer
persuading a jury to convict or acquit.

"William Jennings Bryan," Lynn snarled,
his voice almost a sneer, "Wee Willy."
Reaching the far wall, he turned,
paced back across the room, head lowered,
hands clasped behind his back.
"He did more than any other man
to transform the Democratic party
into the stronghold of liberalism
we've come to identify with FDR, JFK, LBJ
and all their descendants since."
He turned on his heel, paced back the other way.

"Liberals," Jeremy Babcock mocked
under his breath, as if cursing,
his lip curling with disgust.

Blinded Ambition

Two years later Willy set his sights on the Senate.
In Congress the Democrats looked to Willy
to advocate the income tax.
He spoke all over the country,
ran political errands on behalf of cronies,
wrote eloquent arguments,
became a national figure:
now we all claimed acquaintance with Bryan,
now it was a mark of personal prestige
to say we knew him as a boy in Salem.
I dined well at political banquets,
a journalist for the *Sentinel,*
on my borrowed stature, ersatz status,
inflated claims of acquaintance.
I imagined Charlotte, in St. Louis,
eating her heart out, kicking herself
for leaving me for the likes of Lynn.

But Willy lost the race for Senate.
He won three quarters of the popular vote –
meaningless since the legislatures picked the reps –
and since Nebraska's was Republican – both houses –
Willy didn't stand a chance.
He'd never win another election,
just like his daddy.
Who'd have guessed that, then?

Mary's Request

The day after they found out
Willy'd been defeated for the Senate,
we heard a rumor around the newsroom
Mary'd asked her husband
to retire from politics,
a fighter hanging up his gloves.

"You can make a comfortable living,"
Mary argued, urging Willy
to concentrate on his law practice,
devote himself to his writing,
stop traveling around the nation
like a spokesman on a political mission.

But Willy turned her down.
"It would seem to me," he reflected,
"I was born to this life.
I must continue to fight
the battles of the people,
for what I think is right and just,
if I have to do so single-handed
and alone.
I care not whether I am ever
elected to an office or not."

(*Oh yeah? Is that right?*)

God bless her,
Mary devoted herself to her husband's wishes.

The Panther

I almost felt sorry for him losing the election,
but then the bastard muscled in on my territory,
journalism. Gil Hitchcock appointed him
editor-in-chief of the *Omaha World-Herald*
just like that! No experience at all.
Maybe he thought he stood for the people,
but Willy was one of the privileged indeed.

He wrote short editorials,
promoting his political agenda,
continued his public-speaking,
a regular at Chautauqua meetings:
he had the air of a man biding his time,
like a panther waiting to strike,
maneuvering the Democratic party
away from Grover Cleveland's control.

Willy turned thirty-five in March, 1895,
eligible, now, to be president of the nation,
looking, to me, like he was ready to pounce.

Cross of Gold

The Silver Dagger

With the relish of conspiracy theorists,
silver advocates talked about
the "crime of Seventy-three,"
when the silver dollar was dropped
like a stone from the currency,
only to be restored
by "Silver Dick" Bland five years later.

Silver Dick was a hero;
smart money picked him to run for president;
he was Willy's model
for taking over the Democratic party,
forging an alliance between the West
and the South on the money issue.
"We simply say to the East,
take your hands out of our pockets
and keep them out,"
Willy told a cheering Kansas City crowd,
taking a stand for debtor farmers.

Willy spoke all over the West and South,
brandishing the silver message
like a sword of righteousness,
courting Democrats, Populists
and Silver Republicans,
working to ensure
there'd be a majority of silver delegates
at the party's 1896 convention,
for a showdown
with the forces of Grover Cleveland.

Conventional Wisdom

I arrived in Saint Louis for the Republican convention,
there as a reporter for the *Salem Sentinel,*
sure I'd see Charlotte walking
arm in arm with the man
she'd left me for a dozen years ago,
but I was spared.

Instead, I found Willy,
come to the convention representing the *World-Herald*
to witness William McKinley's coronation.
He shook my hand as a colleague,
but his eyes roamed the city
for more important men,
feigning an interest when I reminded him
of our days in Salem.

When the Colorado delegation stormed
from the convention hall
and out of their party
over the adoption of the gold plank,
Willy forgot about me altogether,
watching Senator Teller stalk through the throng,
leading his delegates like Moses
past the parting waters.

Willy was sure now,
as rain gives confidence to a wheat farmer,
he'd be able to unify the silver forces.
He left me standing there
brandishing my pen and notebook,
a bride abandoned at the altar,
running after the retreating delegates
as if wooing other lovers.

Showdown

The *Sentinel* sent me to Chicago, too,
to cover the Democrats, a convention
full of backstabbing political drama.
For starters, Grover Cleveland's
National Committee gave Nebraska's seats
to a rival delegation supporting the gold standard.
Willy had to wait until the convention opened
for the Credentials Committee report to be passed
before he could take his seat.

Then came the spectacle of the platform debate.
Willy sat on the floor of the convention
sucking a lemon to clear his throat,
while a succession of feeble speakers
tried vainly to sway the convention.
Blustering Senator Hill from New York
condemned the silver platform as
"unnecessary, ridiculous and foolish,"
defending Cleveland's gold policies
with about as much inspiration as a bleating ewe.
Two others followed, failing
to ignite the crowd.

Then it was Willy's turn.
He sprang from his seat,
dashed up to the platform,
raised his right arm
to quiet the crowd.

Cross of Gold

"I would be presumptuous indeed,"
Willy began in that honeyed baritone,
with the effect of Antony following Brutus,
"to present myself against
the distinguished gentlemen
to whom you have listened
if this were a mere measuring of abilities.
This is not a contest between persons.
The humblest citizen in all the land,
when clad in the armor of a righteous cause,
is stronger than all the hosts of error.
I come to speak to you
in defense of a cause as holy
as the cause of liberty –
the cause of humanity."

The crowd rose after every sentence,
moved by Bryan's voice,
only to sit, still as penitents,
when he began a new one.

"Our Silver Democrats went forth
from victory to victory,
until they are now assembled,
not to discuss, but to enter up
the judgment already rendered
by the plain people of this country."
The blue smoke of tobacco
hung like a shroud in the dim hall.
The delegates watched, open-mouthed,
not even smoking their cigars.

"There are two ideas of government.
There are those who believe
that if you only legislate to make
the well-to-do prosperous,
their prosperity will leak through
on those below," he thundered,
his scorn for the rich man's promise
wealth would trickle down like rainwater
to restore the fields of the poor
palpable as the smoky atmosphere.

"The Democratic idea, however,
has been that if you legislate to make
the masses prosperous, their prosperity
will find its way up through every class
which rests upon them.

"You come to tell us that the great cities
are in favor of the gold standard,"
he declared, invoking a vision of Sodom and Gomorrah,
"we reply that our great cities rest
upon our broad and fertile prairies."

If this were not Jesus Christ
up on the podium,
it soon would be.

"You shall not press down
upon the brow of labor
this crown of thorns,"
he cried, raking his hands down
over his temples –
I could almost see the blood trickle.
"You shall not crucify mankind
upon a cross of gold."
He spread his arms briefly,
a man pinned to a stake,
dropped them and left the stage.

Nomination

"Greatest speech I've ever listened to,"
I heard Governor Altgeld shout
over the din into Clarence Darrow's ear.
The Illinois governor had been a Bland man
up to the moment Willy bounded to the stage.

The convention delegates stampeded to Bryan
like spooked cattle in a lightning storm.
Bland was the pick in pre-convention polls,
but he withdrew on the fifth ballot,
once he saw how things were going,
and Willy took the prize.

Only thirty-six years old,
youngest presidential candidate ever,
a record that still stands.

I'd like to freeze that moment
when Willy accepted the nomination,
capture that time and put it
behind glass, preserved in amber,
that moment of his greatest triumph,
that lofty peak to which he had risen
and would never,
ever,
see again.

On the Stump

I covered Willy's speeches
in Springfield and Bloomington,
two of the six hundred he delivered
around the nation during the 1896 campaign,
while McKinley stayed home in Canton, Ohio,
and let his machine do the talking for him.

Marcus Hanna ran McKinley's campaign
on about thirty times the money Willy had,
sending out so many pamphlets, posters and buttons
Teddy Roosevelt scoffed they advertised McKinley
"as if he were a patent medicine."

The people greeted Willy that day in Springfield
with delirious shouts of "Sixteen to one!" –
his proposed silver to gold ratio,
sixteen women in white dresses and one in yellow
escorting him out of the station,
each bearing bouquets
with sixteen white roses and one yellow.

Willy's supporters went crazy,
cheering him on like the Savior himself,
while he stood like a statesman
booming his message of prosperity for all
to the adoring crowd.

I stood next to a couple from Decatur
who'd brought their newborn triplets
to see and hear the hero,
the boys named "William," "Jennings," and "Bryan."

"There he is," they pointed at Willy,
as if to a messiah,
the babies not comprehending,
"There's the next president of the United States!"

Election Results

When the returns came in,
I ran into Stumpy Phelps
stumbling out of Turner's Tavern,
drunk to high heaven and sobbing.

"He was robbed! He should of won!
The Republicans bought the election!"
Stumpy was close as a blanket
to the Jennings family.
He'd been going around town bragging
about Willy all that fall
like he was kin.

"Dirty tricks!" Stumpy slurred.
"Those bastards told their workers
to stay home if McKinley lost.
You knew they'd vote their jobs,
too scared to do what's right for the country!"

"Move along, Stumpy," Tom Ryan,
the Salem police officer, said, not too rough.
He'd voted for Willy, too,
even though most of the state went Republican.

"Twenty thousand votes!
God damn it, twenty thousand votes!"
Stumpy's anguish became operatic,
repeating the calculations,
the shift of a few votes in this state or that
that would have spelled Willy's victory.

"God damn it, Stumpy!" Tom barked,
losing his temper. "He lost fair and square.
Quit cryin' about it like a little baby!"

Schadenfreude

I voted for him –
Couldn't bring myself to cast a ballot
for that tub of lard McKinley –
but I took a bit of vindictive
satisfaction from Willy's failure.

"You knew him, didn't you?"
Cletus De Courcy said over a beer
one evening at Turner's.
Clete was new in town,
come from Cairo to work for the *Sentinel*.

"Willy Bryan?" I snorted,
nearly choking on my beer,
about to wave the suggestion away
like a bad smell,
when suddenly I thought,
Sure, I *did* know Willy,
charmed by the notion.

"We weren't real close friends,"
I qualified, my mild denial
sparking a false image
of an acquaintance that never existed,
remembering his daddy Silas' sneer –
a drunk. It still stung all these years later.

"Think of it," Clete marveled,
shaking his head,
"You knew the man
who might have been president."

"Might still be,"
I remarked,
basking in vicarious fame,
hating myself for it.

The Gadfly

In defeat, Willy created a precedent,
cabling his congratulations to McKinley,
the gracious loser, a role he'd play again
and again. And he continued to be the critic,
refusing to give an inch.
"If we are right, we shall yet triumph!"
The fatalistic declaration
like a belief in a heaven
to which you go after death
when you know all along
nothing awaits but the grave.

He and Mary wrote a book together,
The First Battle, all about the campaign,
the history of the silver movement,
his travels across America.
A compilation of speeches, mainly,
fine print, tedious prose.
Ah, who could read it?

Yet it sold like lemonade on a July day;
he donated half the profits
to the silver cause.
You could tell from the tone
and the title alone,
he wasn't conceding an inch.

Mary's loving biographical sketch
made me jealous all over again:
The first time she met him,
his first political speech,
the language of virgins.
He may not have the White House,
but at least he had her.
All I had:
beer and argument at Turner's,
and the memory of a girl I'd lost.

The House on D Street

The *Sentinel* sent me to Lincoln
to write a feature story
on Salem's famous native son,
his life in genteel retirement
from the bare-knuckle world of politics.

Willy supported a huge household
with his prolific pen and silver tongue,
writing and lecturing around the nation,
a sort of snakeoil charmer
with the convictions of an evangelist.

In fact, when I got off the train
in Lincoln that cold early Spring afternoon,
after the endless trip across snowy
stubbled cornfields waiting to be plowed,
and walked to the house on D Street,
I learned that WJ,
as Willy had taken to calling himself,
had gone with Mary to Kansas City
to speak to a silverite convention,
leaving me to scramble for something
to wire back to the editor.

The Two-Sided Desk

I interviewed neighbors, talked to shopkeepers,
toured the Bryan home,
graciously guided by a maid.
The children, ranging in age
from seven to twelve, spilled
down the stairs and into the yard,
politely pausing to be introduced
to "a man who knew your father"
when he was their age in Salem.
But the name Jefferson Powers
meant nothing to them.

Mary's father, John Baird, blind now,
sat in a parlor chair,
a shawl around his shoulders
against the chilly draughts seeping
through the walls like restless spirits,
either napping or praying –
Mr. Baird, I mean, of course.

What stuck most in my mind,
in the center of WJ's study,
like a huge rock jutting up
from the smooth surface of a tranquil lake,
an enormous two-sided desk
where Willy and Mary worked together.
In my mind I saw them there,
heads bent over manuscripts,
and once again the heartbreak
of Charlotte's leaving swallowed me up,
always coming as a surprise,
though how could I ever forget?

Professor Lynn and the Wizard of Oz

"You did know, didn't you,"
Professor Lynn began his lecture
once we'd all settled into our seats,
notebooks open, ballpoints poised,
"L. Frank Baum satirized Bryan
in *The Wizard of Oz*?"

We all looked astonished,
glancing furtively around at our classmates.
Was Lynn joking again?
We all knew the Judy Garland movie.
We'd seen it over and over again as kids.
But Lynn was always twitting us with our lack
of knowledge and sophistication,
Doctor Pee-Aitch-Dee from Princeton
bringing enlightenment out to the prairie hicks.

"The Cowardly Lion – rhymes with 'Bryan.'
He was considered a coward
for opposing the war with Spain,
and later he was a pacifist Secretary of State
in the Wilson administration during World War One.
But just like the lion –
you remember Bert Lahr, don't you?"
Here he danced a little jig,
crooned tunelessly, "Who put the *ape* in *apricot?*"
We all giggled. –
"Bryan *really was* courageous.
He dared to take on the trusts."
Lynn left his notes at the lectern,
commenced his usual metronomic pacing.
"Or maybe he was the Wizard after all,
just another windbag politician from Nebraska."

WJB on Maine and Spain – and Ill-Gotten Gain

McKinley was a decent chap, after all,
at least as far as war went.
He put his money on diplomacy
even as the yellow journals –
ah, my own hometown *Salem Sentinel* among them –
stirred up the nation with lurid images
of Spanish barbarism and atrocities.
Those warmongers in the government,
Senator Henry Cabot Lodge, Teddy Roosevelt
and the rest, beat their chests,
wrapped themselves up in the flag,
slobbered like hungry dogs
over the raw meat of patriotism.
"The Maine was sunk
by an act of dirty treachery
on the part of the Spaniards!"
Roosevelt thundered, an Old Testament prophet
exhorting the Hebrews to justice.

But finally I had to support the war, too,
"Humanity demands that we shall act,"
I conceded. "Cuba lies
within sight of our shores,
and the sufferings of her people cannot be ignored
unless we, as a nation,
have become so engrossed in money-making

as to be indifferent to distress.
War is a terrible thing
and cannot be defended
except as a means to an end."

War Is a Terrible Thing

"Democrats!" Bart Metcalf barked,
leaning on the bar next to me.
"They killed the Union soldiers,
now they won't stand up
to help the Cubans shuck off Spain."

Only a month ago Bart shot
his loud mouth off here at Turner's,
shouting out how the lazy Cubans
weren't worth the effort.
But now that McKinley'd asked Congress
for authorization to intervene,
he whistled a different tune.

"Wee Willy Bryan's poor heart bleeds
for the poor oppressed Cubans,
but now McKinley wants to step in,
he's cautious as a pussycat."

"All's he said was war's serious business,
a terrible thing only justified as a means
to a humanitarian end.
He knows that greedy bastard McKinley
don't care about no Cuban independence,
just wants them and the Philippines for himself."

"Well what's Wee Willy expect?
He think God's gonna come down,
save them like Hebrews
crossing the parted Red Sea?"

"At least he ain't just
shootin' off his mouth in a bar.
He's volunteered for the army.
I hate the way you Republicans act
like you got sole claim to patriotism."

I headed for the door,
wondering if I should volunteer, too,
but hell, Willy and I were both almost forty.
Wasn't it too late for some things by now?
Wasn't it *way* too late?

Willy's War

The day Congress declared war,
Willy wrote to McKinley:
"I hereby place my services
at your command
during the war with Spain."

But instead of blood and guts patriotism,
Willy saw war as a moral last resort,
lest we acquiesce as cowards
to "cruelties which would have been a disgrace."

At the *Sentinel*, we beat our chests
along with the rest of the outraged press,
sneered at Willy for dwelling
on the sufferings of war,
his kneejerk Bible quotes,
"swords shall be beaten into ploughshares,"
envisioning the time when
"justice is enthroned throughout the world."

Willy joined the army as a colonel,
head of Nebraska's Third Regiment,
the "Silver Third," we dubbed it in the press.
Nothing as heroic as Roosevelt's Roughriders,
they traveled down to Florida,
Camp Cuba Libre on the St. Johns River,
where they were ravaged by typhoid and malaria.

The War over Imperialism

Already I could see a political blunder
when Willy demanded we leave
the Philippines and Puerto Rico
to their God-given independence,
just as we were doing with Cuba.

McKinley supported annexation
of Hawaii, Guam, Puerto Rico, the Philippines,
and shrewd Henry Cabot Lodge noted
nobody wanted to hand the islands back to Spain.

Yet Willy mocked Manifest Destiny,
traveling around the country warning
about the evil of imperialism.
It violated the sacred commandments:
Thou shalt not covet; thou shalt not steal;
thou shalt not bear false witness.
Thou shalt not kill.

On Washington's birthday in 1899,
a speech I covered for the *Sentinel,*
Willy nailed his coffin a little further shut.
Manifest destiny, he thundered, is
"the last resort of imperialists
who cannot reconcile colonial policy
with our principles of government."

I found I no longer envied him.
Now, I'd begun to pity him.

Renomination

Nobody wants to stick with a loser,
especially one who champions unpopular causes.
The Democrats flailed about
looking for an alternative in 1900.
First one and then another
dubious politician was flogged
by the party as the ideal candidate,
but their stars flared and fizzled –
Arthur Pue Gorman, a Maryland pol, then
Augustus Van Wyck from the New York machine
inspired the insiders, only to fade
into a bland disenchantment.

They looked about for war heroes
to rally the party around.
Admiral George Dewey, champion
of the Battle of Manila Bay,
the hero who crushed the Spanish fleet
without losing a man or ship.
The New York politician Perry Belmont,
 whose scandalous marriage people still
whispered about – marrying Henry Sloane's ex
only five hours after her divorce was decreed –
sneered, "Admiral Dewey's nomination
would be a glorious ending
to the dead issues of 1896."
Class warfare, of course, and silver
"relegated to the limbo of busted shades."

But Dewey collapsed, and the other war heroes
the pols trotted out – General Nelson Miles,
Admiral W.S. Schley – likewise fell flat.

So the Democrats nominated Willy in Kansas City.
Of course, he'd worked for it,
but when his law partner Dolph Talbot congratulated,
"You're nominated, old man! You're nominated!"
Willy only muttered, "I fear this is too sudden.
If congratulations were based on sound judgment,
November would be a good time to extend them.
So the *Omaha World Herald* reported,
and so did I in *The Salem Sentinel.*

In God We Trust

Willy spoke out against trusts
more than on any other issue that year.
The monopolies they bred threatened liberty,
he warned, over and over again.
Price-fixing, holding companies, all the gimmicks
throttled competition, imperiled small businesses.
When you eliminate competition, he lectured,
prices are controlled
"not by reason but by greed."

I ate it all up, ran stories in *The Sentinel*.
I was afraid I was starting to sound soft,
just another of Willy's acolytes.

All trusts, without exception, should be condemned,
he declared. No such thing as "good" and "bad" trusts.
"There can be no good monopoly
in private hands," Willy cautioned,
"until the Almighty sends us angels
to preside over the monopoly."

As usual, of course, Willy offered
Biblical analogies and admonitions.
"Remember now thy Creator," he bellowed
like an old-time prophet,
"in the days of thy youth
and throughout thy entire life."
Like I said, he could have been a preacher.

The Rematch

Times were good in 1900,
the economy on an uptick,
"the full dinner pail" a slogan
Republicans used to woo the workingman.
They warned a vote for Bryan
was to invite a mad bull
into the china shop of prosperity.
Manufacturers told their employees
operations would be suspended
the morning after Bryan's election.

Down at Turner's, Bart Metcalf warned
from the barstool that was his soap box
Willy would destroy America.
The other barflies wrung their hands,
fearing Bart was right.

Hearst and the press slammed him in editorials.
Cartoonists caricatured Willy
as a demagogue, a fakir, a quack,
a two-faced politician, an anarchist.

Willy hammered away at trusts,
but when the smoke cleared,
Willy had lost
by an even greater margin than 1896.
He even lost Nebraska, his home state.

WJB Reflects on His Loss

The reasons I lost the election?
The war, "better times,"
and all that Republican money.

The grim days of the Cleveland depression
long over, all but forgotten,
we needed to stick with McKinley –
the conventional wisdom.

"There is only one issue
in this campaign, friends,"
McKinley's crafty manager, Mark Hanna,
brayed, "and that's 'leave well enough alone.'"

Victory in the Spanish-American War
made everybody proud, patriotic,
the empire expanding,
America flexing its muscles,
beating its chest.
We'd beaten Spain, taken her islands.

And of course the bastards outspent us
fifty to one. Corporate contributions
to McKinley's campaign
made our war chest a joke,
Hanna a genius at sucking at Wall Street's tits.

But I like to think my old IC prof,
H.K. Jones, hit the truest mark
when he said
I was ahead of the times,
America newly fallen in love
with wealth and power,
like some star-struck debutante,
led astray from the worship of God.

Blood on His Hands

Less than a year after McKinley's re-election
the anarchist, Leon Czolgosz,
gunned the president down
as he shook hands with hundreds
in the reception line
at the Pan-American Exposition in Buffalo.
His revolver hidden under a handkerchief
he held in his right hand,
Czolgosz plugged McKinley twice
just as the President offered his hand.

"Am I shot?" McKinley gasped,
just as bewildered as the crowd.
He slumped forward like a punched
sack of flour, gushing blood.
He died eight days later.

The yellow journals shrieked:
"If Colonel Bryan and others of his stripe
had not made so many speeches
stirring up class hatred...."

"That bastard! That God-damned bastard!"
Euclid Dunham blubbered down at Turner's.
"I bet he's *glad* this happened!
I bet Bryan's happy about it!"

Bart Metcalf just sipped his beer,
shoulders slumped, stared straight ahead,
stony-faced,
while Euclid sobbed beside him.

Jefferson Lynn Lectures about TR and WJB

"When we think of the Progressive Era,
we always think of Teddy Roosevelt,
the Square Deal, economic
and social reforms,
the Interstate Commerce Commission,
regulated railroad rates, workplace safety
measures, maximum working hours laws,
model social welfare practices in DC,
et cetera, et cetera.
Even the national parks.

"Of course, all of these measures
had been in Bryan's portfolio of reforms
long before Roosevelt even dreamed of them.
You could say he stole Bryan's thunder.
You could say Bryan
was ahead of his time.

"But listen," Doctor Lynn commanded us,
and he stopped his hypnotic strutting
up at the lectern, spun
on his heel and stared us down.
"It's not so much that History
is written *by* the winners.
It's that History is written
about the winners."

The Great Commoner Unbound

After his second defeat,
Willy was unfettered by political restraint,
toured the country like a barnstorming evangelist
giving public lectures.
He wouldn't be the main draw
on the Chautauqua tour,
filling tents and town halls,
for several more years,
but his lecture circuit took him
from New York to Philly to Norfolk, VA,
Tennessee, Kentucky, Michigan and Indiana,
Harvard, Princeton, state universities
and scores of smaller colleges.

Willie immersed himself in crowds
of common people, drawing inspiration
from them, speaking with passion
about moral responsibilities in public affairs,
and when Roosevelt took over the presidency,
Willy's favorite topic was his concern
over the trumpeting of military virtues.

And he started a newspaper, too,
editor-in-chief of *The Commoner*,
a weekly full of his opinions, views, speeches.

Younger brother Charley managed *The Commoner* –
subscription lists, printing schedules, correspondence,
layouts and the like.
I hadn't seen Charley since he was a tyke
back home in Salem.
Always devoted to his big brother,
Charley gave up his job as a traveling salesman
to further Willy's political interests,
though later he'd be governor of Nebraska
and even run for Vice President.

The Commoner wasn't copyrighted,
so newspapers could use anything there.
I confess we reproduced lots of Willy's words
in *The Salem Sentinel*.
And we were proud to do it.

Public Enemy Number One

Willy took special aim at John D. Rockefeller,
among all the titans of the trusts –
the Carnegies, the Fricks, the Drews –
those "enemies of government and civilization."
Even if they spent some of their wealth
on good causes, it didn't matter: they were *evil*.

"No criminal now incarcerated for larceny
has shown more indifference to human rights
and property than Rockefeller,"
you could hear him roar in lecture halls.

"Does it lessen his sins that he has given
liberally to churches and colleges?
No, it exaggerates them!
For he attempts to make others
share with him the odium his conduct merits,"
Willy scolded in *The Commoner*,
"for it buys their silence."

Willy went on a tirade against the trusts
in his speeches and *Commoner* editorials.
The trusts, the financial system, imperialism –
All just legitimized larceny.
Sin, sin, sin.

European Tour

Willy and his son William Junior,
fifteen at the time,
went on a European tour.
Mary stayed behind in Nebraska,
thinking she was pregnant – though she wasn't.

"How I miss you, sweetheart,"
Willy wrote his wife as the *Majestic*
pulled out of New York Harbor.
"There is no one else in all the world
to whom I can unbosom myself
and tell all my plans and ambitions –
no one who can be as you are,
a part of myself."

So while Willy went to England and the continent,
had private interviews with Prime Minister Balfour
and other heads of state,
conferred with Tolstoy about peace,
passive resistance, Christian ideals,
as they rode horseback through the countryside
on Tolstoy's estate near the village of Yasnaya Polyana,

I went to Saint Louis to learn what I could
about Charlotte Biggs Powers Lynn.
Like Willy and Mary, they were parents,
but just one boy, Joseph,
younger than Ruth and Willy Junior,
but born the year before Grace Dexter,
Willy's and Mary's last child.

Now I really felt lonesome.
There'd be nobody to mourn
or even remember *me* when I died.

The Rise of Roosevelt

"I am not planning for another
Presidential nomination," Willy'd declared.
"If I were I would not be editing a paper."

When he took over from McKinley,
Teddy'd promised he would
"continue absolutely unbroken"
the slain president's policies –
all conservative, favored by Wall Street.

But when 1904 came around,
Roosevelt rode the Progressive wave,
stole Willy's thunder,
initiated his Square Deal program.

Willy campaigned for Alton Parker –
not with a lot of enthusiasm –
asserting Roosevelt "stands for the spirit of war,"
the Democrats for "peace, reason and arbitration
rather than force, bluster and conquest."

Roosevelt won in a landslide,
winning everywhere but the South.

Chautauqua

"Bryan was what you might call a rock star
on the Chautauqua tour, the summer adult ed. movement
that flourished in rural America up through the twenties.
He was the biggest star, the headliner,
for nearly twenty years, from 1904 on,"
Professor Lynn mused, perched on the classroom desk,
in the small, cozy Friday discussion section,
rather than the cavernous lecture hall
where we met Monday and Wednesday mornings.
"Who are the big acts these days?
The Rolling Stones? The Grateful Dead?"

"The Stones are relics," Jeremy Babcock smirked.
"Mick Jagger's a great-grandfather, and the Dead
haven't been around since Jerry Garcia died
twenty years ago, before I was even born, sir."

"Who then? Lady Googoo?"

The class laughed at how square Lynn was,
even though most of us knew
this was just part of *his* act.

"Bryan began his road show blasting the gold standard
and by the end, a couple decades later,
he was skewering Darwin and his disciples.
People flocked to his lectures.
One impresario noted Bryan was good
'for forty acres of parked Fords, anywhere,
at any time of the day or night.'"

Lynn consulted a notecard.
"There's a story his train was derailed
thirty miles from Sioux Falls.
Bryan hired a horse and buggy
and got there five hours later.
The whole crowd was still there,
and they stayed until after two in the morning
enraptured by Bryan's lecture.

"His most popular lectures?
'The Prince of Peace,' in which
he describes Christian theology
as the foundation of morality,
and 'The Value of an Ideal,'
basically a call to public service.

"All that's gone the way of the sword swallower
and the tightrope walker," Lynn sighed.
"Now we have television.
Now we have Facebook."

Tainted Money

Willy was like a terrier
snapping at the heels of the demon plutocrats.
He made headlines lambasting the ties
between corporate wealth and the academy,
all framed in his simplistic
"Good" versus "Evil" rhetoric.

Of course, we were guilty at the *Sentinel,* too,
sensationalizing Willy's moralistic tirades,
but he *was* a local boy, after all.

Rockefeller he called "an odious eminence,"
condemning a gift to the University of Nebraska
earmarked for a new building,
and when his own alma mater, Illinois College,
on the brink of financial collapse, dared
seek funds from philanthropical Andrew Carnegie,
he practically had a heart attack.
"Our college cannot serve God and Mammon,"
he wrote, swearing that by accepting the gift,
the college commended itself to "commercial highwaymen."

"I had no sympathy
with Mr. Bryan's doctrine of tainted money,"
the Illinois College president reminisced years later;
the gift left the college "perfectly free
to act according to conscience and principles."
The Carnegie aid, he went on,
"saved Illinois College from extinction."

Willy got the news in Hong Kong
that the college had accepted the dirty money,
having embarked with his family
on a trip around the world.
He cabled his resignation from the board of trustees.
"It grieves me to have my Alma Mater
converted into an ally of plutocracy."

Fool's Gold

A Trip Around the World

"You have the contest of your life before you,"
Willy wrote to President Roosevelt
in his farewell letter, promising
"to render you all the assistance in my power."
The whole family left San Francisco Bay
aboard the *Manchuria,* in September, 1905.

Mary's father having died in May,
Willy thought the travel would ease her grief,
and besides, the journey was completely underwritten
by Hearst and other newspaper publishers –
even the *Sentinel* kicked in,
not that I got to make the trip –
Bryan contracted to write articles about the trip.

The Bryans sailed to Japan, then Korea, China, the Philippines,
Borneo, Java, Ceylon, Burma.
They were in the Holy Land by spring,
and on to Damascus, Cairo, Athens, Constantinople,
Vienna, Berlin, St. Petersburg, Norway,
making London by the Fourth of July.

In London speeches, Willy condemned imperialism,
celebrated the ideal of world peace, deplored
"intolerable expenditures on armaments."

Finally, sweeping through Switzerland,
Italy, France, Spain, the Bryans departed
from Gibralter on the *Princess Irene*
late in August, New York-bound,
arriving home in time for school,
the fall mid-term elections,
and the start of the 1908 election cycle.

Me? I traveled once to St. Louis,
but I lost my nerve to talk to Charlotte.
Would she even remember me?

The Men from the Press Said We Wish You Success

"Jesus, can't he at least close the door?"
the *Tribune* reporter muttered.
Years of hard eating and rushing about
had had their effect on Willy –
a bulging waistline, puffy cheeks;
gone the athletic build and the once-wavy black hair,
a shiny bald pate in its place.
He drank large amounts of water with his meals –
doctor's orders – and often scuttled in a hurry to the john,
not always bothering to close the door.

"Bryan's mellower and sweeter," Creelman,
the New York *Herald* reporter who'd covered
the feud between the Hatfields and McCoys
and once interviewed Sitting Bull, remarked.
No longer caricatured as the great bogeyman
stirring up class hatred and anarchism;
the press now saw him as an evangelical missionary.

"How can they be expected to despise in Bryan
what they have applauded in Roosevelt?"
an editorial in *The Nation* demanded.

Watching Willy zip up in that Omaha diner,
damp spots on his trousers, then wash his hands,
I crowded in front of the squeamish *Tribune* hack.
"Mister Bryan," I gushed. "You're advocating
an eight-hour workday, arbitration for labor disputes
and a national income tax?"

"And you are?" he asked, putting a moist hand on my arm.

"Jefferson Powers, *Salem Sentinel*.
 I knew your daddy, Silas."

I didn't register in his eyes.
"Well, Mister Powell, I think those are fine ideas.
I think we should certainly consider them."

The Squarest Christian

"He's the squarest Christian I ever knew,"
Bryan's neighbor Jim Wheeler praised
when I interviewed him for the *Sentinel*
about his illustrious neighbors.
The Bryans'd moved to a farm
four miles outside Lincoln in 1902,
an estate they called Fairview,
Ruth practically grown by then,
the youngest, Grace, just ten.
"When my pasture give out on me,
he said, 'Why, I've plenty, Jim,
just turn your cows in with mine.'"

Willy shunned the Country Club,
looking down on its bar and cocktails,
joining the Farmers' Club instead.
They'd host the meetings in turn,
neighbors bringing chicken fricassee
or mince and custard pies,
and Willy'd sit down at the piano,
lead the gathering in his favorite hymns,
his rich baritone booming through the room:

I'll go where you want me to go, dear Lord,
Over mountain or plain or sea;
I'll say what you want me to say, dear Lord;
I'll be what you want me to be.

Wheeler told me Pentecostal Hymn Number Three,
"I'll Go Where You Want Me to Go,"
was Willy's favorite. Me?
I'd *much* rather have been
over at the Country Club, sipping whiskey.

Three Strikes

I really thought Willy had a chance in 1908.
Taft, Roosevelt's hand-picked successor,
was as drab as those three-piece suits he wore,
that waxy handlebar mustache,
that beer-keg body.

The Panic of 1907, which raged on
into 1908, didn't help Republicans, either.
Stock prices plummeted, production fell,
corporations went bankrupt, banks closed.
Willy advocated for banking regulations,
a system to guarantee bank deposits,
like the one he'd help devise for Oklahoma.

He fought for government aid to the unemployed.
"We must meet an immediate need immediately,"
he thundered in a speech at Cooper Union,
"furnishing labor if labor can be furnished,
giving work if government can supply it,
and giving aid if work cannot be supplied."

Willy courted the labor vote, vowed
to create a Department of Labor in his Cabinet,
wooed the solid Republican black vote,
even won an endorsement from W.E.B. Du Bois.
Even the Eastern newspapers were friendly this time.
Crowds flocked to his speeches.
Everyone thought him running ahead of Taft.
Even the minister of Taft's relatives in Cincinnati
declared he'd vote for Bryan,
since Taft was a Unitarian, "not a Christian."

So I couldn't believe it, spending
half of election night in the *Sentinel* offices,
the other half down at Turner's drowning my disbelief:
Taft crushed him by a million votes
and 321 to 162 where it counted most.

Willy's 1908 campaign slogan?
"Let the People Rule."
And boy, they sure did.

The New York *Times* wrote his obituary:
"For Mister Bryan this is annihilation."

"My only regret," Will consoled his daughter Grace,
sweet sixteen now, nearly grown,
"is that your mother will never be the First Lady,
as she has always been for me."

Temperance

Burt Metcalf belched, lowering his face
to the bar, resting his head
on his folded arms, like a schoolkid,
looked up at me sideways.

"So he's back on the temperance kick, huh?
The sneaky son of a bitch."

"Well, it's only Nebraska politics.
What he does out there won't affect us here in Salem."
I signaled to Hayward, the bartender at Turner's,
to bring us another round.

"The Commoner," Burt sneered, belching again.
"Got licked three times,
but he still wants to muck it up.
He don't know when to quit.
I don't trust the little snake." He snorted.
"Little, hell, he's about as fat as me."

"It's just politics, Burt," I reassured.
"The dry movement's gaining momentum all over.
He's trying to get a lock on the Nebraska Democrats.
He's got his eye on 1912.
But he always *was* a teetotaler."

"A conniving little bastard," Burt muttered.
"Just like his daddy, Silas."

Kingmaker

With the Republicans split,
Roosevelt angry at Taft
for dropping his progressive agenda,
knuckling under to the trusts,
Roosevelt even starting his own party
after Taft got himself nominated in Chicago
even though Teddy'd won most of the primaries,
including Taft's own state of Ohio,
the Democrats' chances of taking the White House
looked better than ever.

I wangled a trip to Baltimore
to cover the Democratic convention the end of June.
Willy was there, too, a Nebraska delegate, but also
a reporter for the New York *World*,
like he'd done in Chicago
at the Republican convention a few weeks earlier.
We both had rooms in the Belvedere Hotel,
a few blocks from Baltimore's Washington Monument,
but Willy never let on he knew me.

Smart money was on Missouri's Champ Clark
until Willy, strutting to the platform
while the band played "See the Conquering Hero Comes,"
dropped a bomb, insinuating Clark was owned
by Wall Street and Tammany Hall.

The Sentinel picked up my expenses,
but Willy was hauling in a thousand bucks a day
to write stories for *The World* about controversies
for which he was mostly responsible.

Willy'd been courting Woodrow Wilson, it's true,
but my hunch?
Everybody whispered Mary'd urged her husband
to get the nomination for himself
since it looked like the Democrats' year.
If he could deadlock the convention,
a Mexican standoff between Clark and Wilson,
they might just turn to him again.

But Wilson won the nomination on the forty-sixth ballot.

Two Cats

"If I am elected, what in the world
am I going to do with W.J. Bryan?"
Wilson steamrolled his opponents,
four-hundred thirty-five electoral votes
to Roosevelt's eighty-eight, Taft's eight –
Vermont and New Mexico – but Wilson's popular vote?
A hundred thousand less that Willy got in 1908.

They could make Bryan British ambassador,
exile him to England,
only, The Commoner declined the offer,
holding out for greater influence.

But one of Wilson's allies summed it up:
"Two cats and one mouse can never agree."
A train wreck was inevitable.

But they had to appoint him something,
bring him into the administration,
if only to put a muzzle on his criticism.
And besides, Willy'd campaigned hard for Wilson,
speaking for him all summer on the Chautauqua circuit
and on into the fall campaign.

So they settled on Secretary of State,
which Willy accepted only
after he pointed out that he and Mary objected
to serving alcohol at state dinners,
and Wilson agreed Willy could make peace treaties
central to his foreign policy.

But when I interviewed Arthur Mullen,
a savvy Nebraska pol who'd seen Willy up close,
he warned Wilson was in for trouble.
When the crisis came one day as it surely would,
"Bryan would desert him
and do it in the name of God."

WJB Declares Victory

We got the income tax amendment, number sixteen,
just weeks before I joined the administration,
the fairest tax of all
since it's based on a citizen's ability to pay.

Then in May we got the Seventeenth Amendment,
the popular election of United States Senators,
another progressive cause I've championed for years.
What a joy to be part of government again
after almost twenty years in exile.

President Wilson is in touch with the people,
fully awake to the demands of the times,
and I am a part of this zeitgeist.

With the new Federal Reserve Board
we've made money a function of government,
no longer surrendered to the banks,
and I can lay aside my cross of gold.
These are President Wilson's New Freedoms,
but they've always been my ideas, my goals.

And peace! Above all else, peace!
As Secretary of State I can help bring war
to an end, forever. We will resolve all disputes
on an intellectual plane,
not on the plane of the brute.
The real welfare of the people
will be advanced not by war, but by peace.
The moral progress of the world
is now ours to shape.

Give Peace a Chance

We filed into the Friday History section
like prisoners back from the yard,
silent, heads bowed, passing the warden,
Professor Lynn, feet propped on his desk,
leaning back in his chair.

As if in church, now, we bowed heads
over notebooks, ballpoints ready to go
like strings of rosary beads.

"All we are say-ing is give peace a chance,"
Lynn croaked in a low voice, and then louder:
"All we are saaaay-iiiing
is give peace a chance."

We looked bewildered, ready to laugh
in case Lynn was making one of his snide jokes.
Wasn't that an old Beatles song?

Lynn raised his arms like a choirmaster.
"Aaaallll we are saaaaaay-ing…," he sang,
looking at us all expectantly.

A few voices responded: "Give peace a chance."

"Wee Willy Bryan, pacifist Secretary of State,
two decades out of power,
and he quits after two years. Why?"
Lynn paused, turned on his heel, paced the room.
"The Germans sink the *Lusitania*,
a hundred and twenty-eight Americans die.
True, there's ammunition on board going to the British,
But the Commoner wants the President
to chastise England equally
for setting up a naval blockade prohibiting shipments
of food to starving German women and children.
We must remain neutral, he implores;
We must use our influence to reconcile both sides –
Persuasion instead of force.

"And when that doesn't happen, he resigns."
Lynn shrugged his shoulders, raised his arms,
as if to say, *unbelievable*.
"As Teddy Roosevelt snarled, 'What can you expect
when the Secretary of State lives in the clouds –
no, not in the clouds, in a world of tenth-rate fiction.'"
Lynn chuckled to himself.
"Of course, if Bryan made George McGovern
look like Attila the Hun,
Roosevelt made John McCain look like a peace freak."

"Doctor Lynn?" Kathy Wade's voice squeaked, tentative,
a bird pecking suet.
"What does this have to do with Progressivism?"

Mary Takes It Hard

In Salem, I only heard secondhand
the drama in Washington that June
when Bryan resigned.
Friday the fourth he told Mary he couldn't sign
the president's letter to the Germans.

"Few Americans want our country involved.
If I resign now, it's possible
the real sentiments of the people will surface."

Mary was attending a luncheon
for the Russian ambassador's wife
when Willy broke the news to Wilson
after the Cabinet meeting.

Mary whisked Willy away to Silver Spring,
a quiet Sunday at the home of Senator Lee –
she could see how distraught her husband was –
but Monday when he went to the White House,
Willy could not persuade the President
his note would surely lead to war,
and back at his Calumet Place home,
he composed his note of resignation,
dated the eighth of June.

After Willy's secretary delivered the note,
Mary slunk off to her room,
locked herself in, sobbed hysterically,
bereft as if she'd lost a child,
the first and only time in her adult life.

I couldn't help remembering Charlotte's anguished sobs
all those years ago,
and only wished it had likewise been
for something noble I'd done.

John Reed Interviews The Great Commoner

The hot shot journalist John Reed,
who'd interviewed Pancho Villa in 1913,
now back from the Eastern Front overseas,
traveled down to Florida to interview Bryan
eight months after the Great Commoner's resignation.
Talk about a scoop! If only it were me!

"Bryan on Tour" appeared in *Collier's* in May.
I couldn't get my hands on it fast enough.
"A bourgeois Don Quixote," Reed wrote.
"Politics did not corrupt him;
defeat did not change his way of life."

Reed covered an anti-war speech
at the Palatka Opera House
("firstly, secondly and thirdly like a sermon"),
then Bryan invited him on his yacht,
a fishing trip down the Saint Johns River,
through the dense tropical forest, the swamp,
"cedars draped with Spanish moss, creepers,
tall leaning palms and spiky palmettos."
I salivated, envious. They talked about the war.
Both opposed it, Bryan as an isolationist, a pacifist,
Reed on principles of international socialism.
"Love is the only weapon for which there is no shield,"
Willy told him, preacher-like, "And it must guide nations
to peace, as it guides individuals to peace."

They stopped at Orange Springs Landing;
Willy orated to the several dozen there;
and at Ocala, Bryan "sneered at Darwinian theory,"
claiming it "has done more to paralyze Christian ethics
than any other thing in the world."

They had their differences, but Reed admired him.
"After all, whatever is said,
Bryan has always been on the side of democracy.
Remember that he was talking popular government
twenty years ago and getting called anarchist for it,
remember that he advocated such things as the income tax,
popular election of senators, railroad regulation,
the destruction of private monopoly
when such things were considered
the dreams of an idiot."

He Kept Us Out of War

Willy campaigned for Wilson that fall,
no misgivings between them.
Wilson's campaign slogan?
"He Kept Us Out of War."
The Great Commoner took some credit.

After he left office, Willy went around the country
speaking out against "preparedness" –
the euphemism for the manufacture of armaments –
voicing his contempt for war profiteers and jingoists
intent on sending young American kids to fight.

Wilson won by the narrowest of margins,
but his campaign worked: the anti-war candidate.

Willy spoke throughout the West, denouncing
"The Causeless War," condemning it
in no uncertain terms. Not a contest
between good and evil,
the war only fed on revenge and sacrifice.

At the speech Reed attended at the Palatka Opera House
Willy had thundered, "We have the welfare
of a hundred million people to guard
and priceless ideals to preserve," and we would not
"wallow in the mire of human blood
just to conform to a false standard of honor."

American Zeitgeist • Rammelkamp — 113

Aspiring to the role of mediator, the great
neutral peacemaker, Wilson declared to the Senate,
"Only a peace between equals can last,"
and he proposed the foundation of the League of Nations.

But only two weeks later when the Germans announced
they would resume their campaign against merchant ships,
Wilson broke off relations with Germany.

War

"He stopped being a pacifist
when Congress passed the war resolution in April,"
I corrected Burt Metcalf,
half in his cups at Turner's,
spouting about Bryan's cowardice, hinting at treason.

"He sent a telegram to Wilson
offering himself as a private in the army?"
Burt sneered. "Pathetic."

"I didn't see you volunteering. Or myself for that matter."

"And you *won't* see me volunteering, neither!
For Christ's sake, Jeff, we're old men.
And so is Wee Willy Bryan. Pure grandstanding."

"Well, he's talking about 'extreme sacrifices.'
I think he just wants to inspire citizens by example."

"He don't inspire *me*, I can tell you.
Wilson didn't take him up on it, of course.
So then didn't he write the Secretary of War
and offer to be an assistant chaplain?
At least that's more his speed.
But Baker didn't want him neither!"
Burt took a swig of beer,
wiped his mouth on his sleeve.
"Reminds me of the time *Colonel* Bryan
moved the Third Regiment to Savannah
during the Spanish War twenty years ago
and immediately gets malaria!" Burt scoffed,
shaking his head. "*Colonel* Bryan."

"It was typhoid," I corrected again.
"You're right, he's no Teddy Roosevelt,
but he's a genuine man of peace, Burt."

What It Means to Be Patriotic

"Kept us out of the war, my ass,"
Ellison Jordan wailed over his whiskey.
His boy, Gibbon, drafted into the Thirty-second,
the "Red Arrow" Division made up mostly
of kids from Michigan and Wisconsin,
burnt past recognition by a German *Flammenwerfer*
at the Hindenburg Line near Soissons.

"Well, you voted for Hughes, didn't you?"
Burt Metcalf pointed out. "I sure as hell did.
Most of the state voted for him, too."

"But all for *what*?" Ellison cried,
his anguish like a splintered pane of glass.
"What do those European countries
have anything to do with us, with my son?"

"I'm just saying," Burt consoled.
"Willy Bryan was all fired up
to keep us out of that mess; he had Wilson's ear.
If he hadn't been so stirred up
to close down the saloons –
he must have spoke at least as much
about 'the Demon Drink' as he did
about keeping us out of that war –
I might have voted for Wilson myself.
But that snake called it 'patriotic' to get rid of alcohol –
'Oh, we need all that grain for the war effort,' he says now,
Burt mimicked. 'Seven million acres wasted
on grain for alcohol.' *Waaah-waaah-waaah.*
I could just kick his ass from here to Sunday."

But Ellison didn't want to hear about it.
All he cared about was Gibbon.
I felt so bad for him, I bought them both another round
and headed out of Turner's for the *Sentinel* offices.

Prohibition

"Figures it would be *his* state
put the amendment over the top."
You could see Burt Metcalfe's simmering anger
in the way he grabbed his beer stein,
 as though he were strangling somebody.
Nebraska had just become the thirty-sixth state
to ratify the prohibition amendment.
It would become law in exactly a year.
"God damn that son of a bitch.
If he ever comes back to Salem…."

"Bryan wasn't the only one for it," I pointed out.

"No, but he sure as hell was the loudest.
And he made money off it, too, the snake.
The Anti-Saloon League's been paying him
to make speeches denouncing alcohol.
He writes sermons about it in *The Commoner*.

"Next thing you know his amendment
giving women the vote'll go through."
Burt shook his head sadly at the changing world.

"I've been coming down to Turner's
most of my life, Jeff," he lamented,
as if he had just lost his best friend.
"Now what am I going to do?"

Age and Illness

When I reached the age of sixty,
already three more than my father,
dead from diabetes at fifty-seven,
I too became consumed by health –
mine and Mary's.

Arthritis gripped my dear girl,
so severe she couldn't stand,
walk, dress or undress,
seizures so crippling she shriveled
like a crumpled piece of paper,
bent and aching in her joints,
the pain so great she moaned, whimpered,
slumped low, curled up, fetal,
spent weeks in hospital care.

We took her to Johns Hopkins in Baltimore,
the spas in Hot Springs,
retreated to out Villa Serena in Florida
for ever increasing stays.
We even called in a faith healer,
she felt so desperate.
Sometimes our measures seemed to help,
but others….
Oh, I so hope the Lord will let her
be my companion for the rest of my pilgrimage.
here on Earth.

And me? Lined, bald, slack cheeks,
the strain of ceaseless campaigning,
my speaking schedule have all
taken their toll.

At least I've given up sweets,
much to Mary's relief.
I tried that new drug, Insulin,
said to prolong the lives of diabetics,
but I couldn't keep up the regimen:
my speaking schedule's just too irregular
to fit it in.

Illness and Age

The rigors of journalism have sucked me
empty and slack as a deflated balloon.
Burt Metcalf's death made me reconsider
the hours I keep, the things I eat and drink.
If only I'd had a woman to look after me,
I might have taken better care of myself.
But after Charlotte left, I never met another girl.
Didn't really want to.

A week before Turner's had to close down,
Burt didn't show up one evening.
He'd vowed he'd be the last man
taking a legal drink there, the old cuss.
Nobody thought anything about it,
but when he didn't show up the next night either,
a group of us went to his house.
Burt lived alone on the edge of town.

We found him dead in his bed,
a half-empty whiskey bottle on the table.
Coroner called it a heart attack, said
Burt'd been dead over forty-eight hours.

The Menace of Darwinism

This had to be his last great crusade.
What could possibly follow
taking on Darwin, Nietzsche (who would replace
"the worship of the superman for the worship of Jehovah"),
standing up for God and Christianity?
"I am trying to save the Christian Church,"
he implored, a lover on his knees,
"from those who are trying to destroy her faith."

My goodness, he already had his own mega-church
down in Florida, teaching
his famous Bible class to thousands every Sunday,
his "Bible talks" syndicated in all the newspapers,
including our *Salem Sentinel.*

Now the Great Commoner took on the colleges,
the public school system. Godlessness, he warned,
crowded out moral influences on our kids.
He took his message to college campuses –
Ann Arbor, Providence, Cambridge –
sometimes drowned out by the boos and hisses.
"We cannot afford to have the faith
of our children undermined," he thundered
at Nebraska's constitutional convention.
He urged Kentucky state legislators
to support a bill banning the teaching of evolution
in schools receiving state taxes.

To the West Virginia legislature he cried,
"Evolutionists rob the Savior
of the glory of virgin birth,
the majesty of his deity,
and the triumph of his resurrection."

This was our Willy, all right,
passionate about whatever
was his latest cause.

When I'm Sixty-five

Look at us, we're wrecks.
Mary frets about my diet,
the sugars and the starches she says
are like striking a match to the kindling of diabetes.

But Mary's the one I worry about,
the dear girl wracked by pain, wheelchair-bound.
Look at me – time may have etched its signature
onto the canvas of my carcass,
my flabby belly, my pouchy cheeks,
but I'm still able to lecture,
touring the country with my messages,
"The Menace of Darwinism," "Back to God,"
fighting the scourge of the atheists, the agnostics, the unbelievers,
while she, dear girl, can't even dress herself.

And yet we've been blessed
with such a wonderful, beautiful life together!
"I love you better and better each year,"
she wrote in her birthday greeting,
and I assured her, averring our partnership,
"Our work is not yet done."

And so I sit beside her now,
grandchildren on my knee,
remembering her so vividly that day,
at the open house at the Jail for Angels,
the loveliest young woman in Jacksonville –
the loveliest girl in the whole world!

Local Interest

Of course, I knew the Scopes family –
or I'd heard of them, anyway.
They moved to Salem in 1917
from Paducah, Kentucky, where John was raised,
by way of Danville, up near Champaign.
John graduated from Salem Senior High in 1919,
then went on to Urbana for a year to study at the U of I
before completing his degree at the University of Kentucky,
so I can't say I knew *him* very well.

But even with my precarious health,
there was no way in the world I'd have missed
that trial in Dayton.
It featured a couple of local boys, after all,
and the fireworks promised to be explosive,
a heavyweight fight between Wee Willy in one corner,
Clarence Darrow in the other,
better than Jess Willard and Jack Dempsey.

Darrow and the Great Commoner'd squared off before.
Darrow declined to stump for Bryan in 1908,
saying Bryan was avoiding the dangerous issues,
and in 1910 Darrow stood up
for the rights of men to do as they pleased
when Bryan was on his temperance high horse
denouncing "drink and the nefarious liquor interests."
Darrow'd even taunted him before on evolution,
in an open letter to the Chicago *Tribune* in 1923.

Scopes? He was just a pawn on the chessboard.
He'd agreed to be the ACLU test case of the law
Governor Peay'd signed making it a crime
"to teach any theory that denies the story
of the divine Creation of man as taught in the Bible,
and to teach instead that he was descended
from a lower order of animals."
What did he have to lose?
 The ACLU'd provide legal and financial assistance,
and the Baltimore *Evening Sun* picked up the tab
on his $500 bond.
Besides, John said he was sick of teaching,
wanted to go back to school himself.

Rhea County Courthouse

Somebody described the courthouse
"as though it had been designed by a Congressman" –
a rectangular red brick building
with Romanesque arches,
a three-story tower in one corner,
clocks on all four faces,
topped with a gazebo like a gaudy cake confection.

Even before the trial began that Friday, July 10,
and despite the ferocious southern summer heat,
farmers filled the courthouse, sun-bronzed faces,
clad in their armor of overalls,
here to cheer on their hero,
the defender of God and civilization.

On Sunday, two days later,
only a fortnight before his death,
Willy preached to them from the Methodist pulpit:
"God does not despise the learned," he reminded, but
"the unlearned in this country are much more numerous
than the learned. Thank God
I am going to spend the latter years of my life
in a locality where there is a belief in God,
and in the Son of God,
and in a civilization
to be based on salvation through blood."

Monkey Business

All that first scorching week,
July leaning on us like a schoolyard bully,
the lawyers debated motions and technicalities
like teams on either side of a badminton net
swatting the shuttlecock back and forth.

The farmers called blue-suspendered Darrow "the infidel,"
and soon the press picked it up, with some affection.
Coatless, collarless Bryan, sweating like a pig,
his palm fan at hand, sat by himself
while his prosecution team haggled with the defense.

A few days in, Darrow lit up the placid proceedings.
Shoulder hunched, plucking the strings of his suspenders,
Darrow prowled the arena of the courtroom like a
prizefighter.
"This is as brazen and bold an attempt to destroy liberty
as was ever seen in the Middle Ages!" he thundered,
and when Judge Raulston tried to open court with a prayer,
he objected this would influence the jury.
Bryan flung down his fan,
glowering at his rival.
Let the show begin.

Willy in the Jungle

On Thursday, Willy spoke at last,
his admirers swooning at his oratory.
"This is not the place to try to prove
that the law ought never to have been passed,"
he began, since this was, after all,
a trial about breaking that law.
"The place to prove that was at the legislature."

But sensing his devotees wanted blood,
an assault upon the infidels to send them reeling,
he ignored his partners' advice
and launched into an attack on evolution,
ridiculing Scopes' textbook, *Civic Biology*,
scorning and denouncing that book
from which he had taught his students
"that man was a mammal and so indistinguishable
among the other mammals!"

Willy thundered: "Talk about putting Daniel
in the lions' den! How dare those scientists
put man in a ring with lions and tigers
and everything that is bad?"

The "rustic japes" and "yokels,"
as Mencken called them,
cheered and whooped and laughed
as their hero dug his own grave.

Intermission

Every day was like a round in a heavyweight fight,
one side or the other trying to score points,
looking for an opening to land the haymaker.

On Sunday the court was adjourned,
a week to the day before Willy died.
Darrow lectured on Tolstoy in Chattanooga
to the Young Men's Hebrew Association,
and Willy addressed five hundred of his faithful farmers
in Pikeville, in the Sequatchie Valley,
on "the gigantic conspiracy" of atheists and agnostics
to destroy Christianity, disgrace religion.

And John Scopes?
John went dancing and swimming
at Morgan Springs, carefree as a swallow.

The Monkey House

I only learned later from the other reporters –
Ochs at the *Chattanooga Times* and the *Herald Tribune* man –
about the meeting at the Monkey House,
as we called the rambling residence
where the defense counsel stayed,
on that same Sunday evening,
with Darrow, his partner, Arthur Garfield Hayes,
and the Harvard geologist, Kirtley Mather,
where they cooked up the scheme
to get Willy up on the stand,
Mather standing in for Bryan
as they peppered him with questions.

After two hours of practice,
Mather asked, "How in blazes
do you expect to get Bryan on the witness stand?"

"Leave that part to us,"
Darrow's smiling reply.

Humiliation

It was so hot in that courthouse,
at the urging of the fire commissioner,
Judge Raulston moved the trial
out to the courthouse lawn,
not that it provided a great deal of relief
from that smothering July heat,
but he warned the floor might give way,
the plaster already cracking downstairs
from all weight of the people in the courtroom.

Outside, Bryan swatted at his face with a fan,
sweat trickling into his collar,
but it looked like they had the defense on the ropes.
Bryan and his partner Dudley Malone –
who'd been an assistant to Willy
when he was Wilson's Secretary of State –
had both spoken against evolution.
everybody there on his side
as he denounced evolution as evil,
and declared they'd "uncovered the conspiracy
against the Bible Christianity."
He'd stood like Cicero, a living monument.

But Darrow had a crafty strategy up his sleeve,
using Willy's jaunty confidence against him.
Outside on the lawn,
Hays called the Great Commoner as a witness.
The whole prosecution team leaped to their feet, objecting.
But Willy, convinced of the righteousness of his cause,
waved them away, consented to testify.
He'd brought the subject up himself already;
now it was his duty to defend his position.

Cocky as an undefeated champ,
sure of his oratorical skills,
Willy walked right into the buzzsaw of Darrow's cross-examination,
Darrow baiting him with questions about the Bible stories,
just as they'd rehearsed the evening before –
God making the sun stand still, the serpent condemned
to crawl on his belly ("Have you any idea
how the snake went before that time?"),
language dating back to the Tower of Babel.

Leaning in toward the dripping Bryan,
still beating the air with his fan,
dried perspiration a sheen on his pale slack cheeks,
crusty old Clarence asked him about the date of the Flood,
his endless questions a torrent sweeping Willy to frustration.
Dismissive, Bryan said he'd never calculated it.

Darrow, elbow on the witness stand, bending in,
asked the Great Commoner, his voice quiet, patient,
"What do you think?"

With the impatience of the preacher unaccustomed
to being questioned, Willy snapped,
"I don't think about things I don't think about."

And then Darrow brought down the house:
"Do you think about things you do think about?"
The courtroom roared, Willy reduced to a buffoon.

Willy Denounces Darrow in the Name of God

The press table howling,
laughter like a wave among the spectators,
Willy leaped to his feet,
shoulders slumped with exhaustion,
the sweat lighting up his face
as he continued to perspire.

"Your honor, the only purpose Mr. Darrow has
is to slur the Bible!" He turned to the crowd.
"I want the world to know that this man,
who does not believe in God,
is trying to use the court of Tennessee –"

"I object to your statement!" Darrow yelled.
He shook his fist at Willy,
the two threatening to come to blows.
"I am examining you on your fool ideas
that no intelligent Christian on earth believes!"

Suddenly it was as if a riot might break out,
red-faced spectators pushing and screaming,
and Raulston brought down his gavel, shouting,
"Court is adjourned until nine o'clock tomorrow morning!"

Fool's Gold

"You have given considerable study
to the Bible, haven't you, Mr. Bryan?"
Darrow began his cross-examination
of my husband, and my heart sank.
I could see the ridicule coming a mile away.

Darrow's colleague, Arthur Hays,
pushy as New York Jews can be,
had shocked the throng of three thousand
on the lawn outside the courthouse,
where the judge had moved the proceedings,
when he announced, "The defense desires
to call Mr. Bryan as a witness."

My poor dear William jumped to the bait,
certain his eloquence could stand up to Darrow's mocking.
Oh, the lure of defending Christianity from heathens,
glittering like false gold before his dazzled eyes!
How I remember the way he moved the crowd
at the Coliseum in Chicago with his Cross of Gold,
and how he persuaded millions of readers
with his reasoned arguments in *The Commoner*.

But he was no match for this circus master.

And then that snob Mencken nailed his coffin shut.
"He seemed like a poor clod like those around him,"
he wrote, "deluded by a childish theology,
full of an almost pathological hatred of all learning."

After

After Darrow made a laughingstock of Bryan,
and we reporters had filed our stories,
the next day the defense asked the court
to give the case to the jury,
the ridiculous image of Bryan now fixed
in the public's awareness, for all time,
and the jury returned a "guilty" verdict
in just a matter of eight minutes.

After the whole world winced at Willy's disgrace,
Bryan never let on he'd been humiliated.
As always, he had a speech written
to assert the righteousness of his cause,
and after the trial he went to Chattanooga
to see about its publication
while we journalists packed up and went home.

McCartney, the Bryans' chauffer, drove Mary
down from Dayton to retrieve her husband.
They returned to Dayton, and on Sunday
Willy led a Methodist congregation in prayer.
Scopes' conviction, he said, was a great victory
for Christianity, and a staggering blow
"to the forces of darkness."

After his Sunday dinner at noon,
and after making arrangements for a vacation
with Mary in the Smoky Mountains,
he went to his room for a nap.
He never woke up.
After that, all hell broke loose.

Charlotte Biggs' Legacy

I was ninety-three when my grandson
Chet and his wife Emily
went to New York to see *Inherit the Wind*
on Broadway, the National Theater.
He was always a William Jennings Bryan buff,
ten years old when The Great Commoner died,
impressed by all that funeral pomp –
Bryan laid in state at "the church of Presidents,"
the New York Avenue Presbyterian Church,
buried a military hero at Arlington.

Our hearts all ached, every one of us sobbing
for that brave widow in the wheelchair,
her frantic sorrow at her husband's sudden death.
Despite her disabilities, she'd complete
her husband's memoirs, a sacred task,
as though the two still
worked across from one another
at that big desk in Fairview.

It made me remember all over again
my first failed marriage.
Dear Jefferson, how I broke his heart,
but three years of late nights,
working all hours at the newspaper office,
obsessing over his classmate's career,
the stink of alcohol and tobacco all over him,
I had to get away the only way I could.

I heard from friends he was found
dead at his desk at *The Sentinel*,
the year the stock market crashed,
almost seventy years old, a lonely old man.

I don't even know if my grandchildren know
their Nana'd been married once before.
Maybe their parents told them in confidence
when they were old enough to know
the strange ways of the heart.

But when I learned Emily'd become pregnant –
probably that week they were in New York –
I asked Chet if he'd consider the name
"Jefferson" for my first great-grandchild.

Footnote

"There'll be a quiz on Friday
on the Progressive Era –
trusts, monopolies, the railroads,
TR, the Square Deal, 'Fighting Bob' La Follette,
and, of course, everybody's favorite,
Wee Willy Bryan," Professor Lynn announced.
"You can use your notes.
Next week we'll start on World War One,
the Roaring Twenties and the Great Depression."

A man in his early sixties, I'd say,
white hair, jaws gone slack,
a thin guy with a little bit of a gut,
Lynn strutted back and forth
in front of the class,
regular as a pigeon,
hands clasped behind him
like a defense attorney summing up.

"In the end, though he ran for president
three times, shaped the Democrats' liberal message,
outlined the Progressive agenda like nobody else,
spoke out against war and imperialism,
he reverted to his holier-than-thou prohibitionism,
made a fool of himself proclaiming Creationism –
which the religious right idiots try to resurrect
even to this day as "Intelligent Design" –
he was just a footnote in our history,
as all losers inevitably are.

"But here's the thing:
my great-grandmother was married once
to a journalist from his hometown, Salem –
same hometown as John Scopes, by the way –
before she left him for my great-grandfather.
Old Jefferson Powers followed Bryan
like his shadow, all around the country,
all down his career,
and my parents even gave me his name!
Jefferson. Jefferson Lynn."
Lynn spun on his feet and stared us down.
"That's *Doctor* ... *Professor* Jefferson Lynn to you!
Class dismissed."

Biographical Note

Charles Rammelkamp was born in Jacksonville, Illinois, in 1952, one of a pair of twins, but he grew up and went to school in Albion, Michigan, where his father taught History at Albion College.

Rammelkamp returned to Jacksonville to attend Illinois College, where he graduated with a BA in Philosophy in 1975. A couple of years later he went to graduate school at Boston University and received an MA in English.

It was in Boston that he met his wife Abby. They moved to Baltimore in 1983. A few years later Rammelkamp earned another MA, this one in Publications Design at the University of Baltimore.

Now retired, Rammelkamp spent his career as a technical writer for various software and information technology organizations, including twenty years at the Social Security Administration. For ten years, too, he was a member of the adjunct faculty in the English Department at Essex Community College where, among other courses, he taught Creative Writing.

During all this, he pursued his own writing, sending poetry and fiction to small literary magazines and journals. He has published a novel (*The Secretkeepers,* Red Hen Press), two collections of short fiction (*A Better Tomorrow,* PublishAmerica, and *Castleman in the Academy,* March Street Press), three previous full-length poetry collections

(*The Book of Life,* March Street Press, *Fusen Bakudan,* Time Being Books, and *Mata Hari: Eye of the Day,* Apprentice House). He has also published several poetry chapbooks – *I Don't Think God's that Cruel, Go to Hell, A Convert's Tale,* and *Mixed Signals.*

Rammelkamp has edited the online literary journal, *The Potomac,* since 2008, and he is the Prose Editor for BrickHouse Books in Baltimore. He has two daughters and one granddaughter.

Apprentice House Press
Loyola University Maryland

Apprentice House is the country's only campus-based, student-staffed book publishing company. Directed by professors and industry professionals, it is a nonprofit activity of the Communication Department at Loyola University Maryland.

Using state-of-the-art technology and an experiential learning model of education, Apprentice House publishes books in untraditional ways. This dual responsibility as publishers and educators creates an unprecedented collaborative environment among faculty and students, while teaching tomorrow's editors, designers, and marketers.

Outside of class, progress on book projects is carried forth by the AH Book Publishing Club, a co-curricular campus organization supported by Loyola University Maryland's Office of Student Activities.

Eclectic and provocative, Apprentice House titles intend to entertain as well as spark dialogue on a variety of topics. Financial contributions to sustain the press's work are welcomed. Contributions are tax deductible to the fullest extent allowed by the IRS.

To learn more about Apprentice House books or to obtain submission guidelines, please visit www.apprenticehouse.com.

Apprentice House
Communication Department
Loyola University Maryland
4501 N. Charles Street
Baltimore, MD 21210
Ph: 410-617-5265 • Fax: 410-617-2198
info@apprenticehouse.com • www.apprenticehouse.com